Dedication

This publication is dedicated to those honest, hard-working laborers, predominantly mountain residents and Civilian Conservation Corps (CCC) of the Depression era, who toiled for as little as thirty cents an hour, and to the brilliant visionaries and dedicated engineers, all of whom endured the bitter cold of mountain winters and oppressive heat of summers to create the visual legacy and haven for environmental preservation that we know as the Blue Ridge Parkway.

The author would like to thank: Patty Lockamy, Chief of Interpretation of the Blue Ridge Parkway; Jackie Holt, curator of the National Park Service's Blue Ridge Parkway Library in Asheville; Karen Searle of Eastern National's Blue Ridge Parkway Region; Sally Council, compiler for *The Blue Ridge Music Trails*; Tina Charlebois, Blue Ridge Parkway District Interpreter for the Cone/Price/ Minerals Museum area; Carlton Abbot; Peter Margolin for his geology expertise; Appalachian author, John Foster West; and Rick Polad.

The Blue Ridge Parkway

To drive the Blue Ridge Parkway is to travel along a scenic highway in the sky; it is an experience with trees, flowers, misty treks, foggy sunrises, vistas and valleys, living geology, mountain music and dance, crafts, and its people. It is the preservation of nature and the conservation of the right to ponder its greatness amidst grand vistas.

The Parkway is a road by and for humanity that follows the crest of the highest mountains on the East Coast through southern Virginia to the Great Smokies in North Carolina. It is the ancient paths and burial grounds of Native Americans, the smell of wood smoke from a nearby cabin, the sound of one's footsteps on a rocky path, the smell of the fresh, cool woods, the scent of fallen trees returning to the earth, the sounds of squirrels scampering up a tree, the plaintive cry of the wood thrush, the velvet touch of a new leaf, the melody of a rushing stream and the cascading waterfall, and the silence of falling snow. It is the opportunity to have thoughts as deep as these woods, as ancient as these mountains, as quiet as time slipping into infinity.

Front cover and Table of Contents photos by Hugh Morton
All photographs not otherwise credited are by Bruce Roberts

Wrinkles in time:
Making of a Mountain Range

Clouds appear as white froth upon a sea of mountains, reminiscent of the ancient ocean that once was here and drained eastward by uplift of the earth to create the Blue Ridge Mountains three-hundred-million-years ago. Modern geology theory states that the collision of the African and North American continental plates formed the Appalachian Mountains. The Blue Ridge Mountains, the eastern escarpment of this chain, is home to the imposing Grandfather Mountain. The tumultuous creation was akin to stacking cards one upon the other when hot rock was lifted up from deep within the earth's furnace, layering newer rock upon older rock. Erosion, over the hundreds of thousands of millennia in the forms of wind, rain, and ice, has exposed original igneous and sedimentary rock. This phenomenon is called the "Grandfather Mountain Window." Rock at Linville Falls, for instance, has been measured at 1.1 billion-years-of-age and 800 million-years-of-age at Grandfather Mountain. Here is proof that beauty and age go hand in hand.
Photo by Hugh Morton

To understand how these gentle giants came into existence, consider the seven major "plates" that make up the crust of the Earth. The movement of these plates, some bearing continents, others ocean floors, has triggered major geologic events such as mountain building.

Geology interpreter Peter Margolin works for the National Park Service at the Museum of North Carolina Minerals. He explained how the Blue Ridge Mountains were formed. "About 300 million years ago, the continent of Africa slammed into the North American plate, and huge sections of the earth's crust were broken into slabs while old rock from deep within the earth was driven up and over newer material, like a load being pushed up and over a ramp. We call such ramps 'faults.'" Margolin made the analogy that the event was like splitting a deck of cards and then shuffling it. "The final effect was similar to shingles, one overlapping another, one sheet pushed up on top of another and on top of another, with faults forming the upper and lower surfaces of each sheet.

"'The Grandfather Mountain Window' is probably the single-most significant geological feature along the Blue Ridge," Margolin shared. "It runs from Boone-Blowing Rock clear down to Linville Falls." As he described it, "The rock sheets are stacked upon one another, and the Grandfather Mountain Window is an opening in those stacked sheets that allows people to see what's under there, including the faults upon which the sheets moved."

The Appalachian Mountains have been affected by several geological events when older rock within the furnace-like depths of the earth were pushed up and over younger material, changing the shape and contents of the mountain rock. Sandstone was metamorphosed into quartzite, for instance. Thus, geologists have had difficulty identifying "original" sedimentary and igneous rock. The geologic significance of the Grandfather Mountain Window is the exposure of "original" rock, over one billion years old in some places.

But a billion years ago there was no Blue Ridge. Today's Appalachians were formed millions of years later. Then, over hundreds of thousands of millennia, the sculpting powers of weathering and erosion artfully carved the curved hills and deep valleys that sweep south from Nova Scotia to Alabama and Mother Nature has provided the luscious flora that covers these rolling mountains. The Blue Ridge Mountains, eastern escarpment of the extensive Appalachians, in North Carolina alone comprise 252 miles of scenic grandeur as displayed in the summits of Grandfather Mountain, the Black Mountains (home of Mt. Mitchell- the tallest peak east of the Mississippi), the Great Craggies, the Great Balsams, and the Plott Balsams.

Margolin commented, "The mountains are still rising, but not as rapidly as weathering and erosion are wearing them down. Streams that cross the Parkway provide the most striking evidence of vigorous erosion, cutting into the rocks and creating gorges and canyons. An example is the James River cutting across the Blue Ridge in Virginia, where the Parkway dips to its lowest elevation, 649 ft above sea level. Even more dramatically, the Linville River has cut Linville Gorge, the deepest and most rugged gorge east of the Eastern Continental Divide."

Margolin also explained the beautiful diversity of trees. "The floral landscape that you see along the Blue Ridge reflects certain events in earth's history that go back thousands of years. The last Ice Age ended 10,000 years ago but, particularly at higher altitudes, the forests that you see here are more typical of New England and Canada than they are the southern Appalachians. That's because during the Ice Age the ice caps only extended as far south as Pennsylvania, Ohio, New Jersey, and New York, but it was a lot cooler and wetter down here, and all that vegetation that would have been growing up there moved down here, ahead of the advancing ice sheet.

"The wind, birds, and other animals dispersed the trees' seeds from the North. The trees took root south of the ice cap- there was no chance that they would take root in an ice cap. Then, when the ice disappeared up there while the climate warmed up again, that northern vegetation could survive here only at the higher altitudes where it is cooler. So that's why, for instance, on Mt. Mitchell there is a spruce-fir forest, which is typical of Canada. And at somewhat lower elevations, there lies a New England hardwood forest of oaks and maples instead of a typically southern softwood," Margolin concluded.

The Blue Ridge Parkway and its frequent scenic overlooks afford the visitor a front-row seat to the southern and highest ridges of the Appalachian Mountains along a leisurely 469-mile, tree-lined scenic drive.

Though this pastoral scene of valley and mountain appears to be static, appearances are deceiving. As you stand gazing out over the serene mountains, beneath your feet dynamic forces, at work since creation, are slowly altering the landscape. The gradual process of erosion performs a balancing act with "uplift," another dynamic force that causes buoyant material deep within the earth to constantly migrate upward toward the surface.

These mountains, wrinkles in time, offer memorable views portrayed in seasonal personalities, calling us to visit again and again and giving us something new and rewarding each time. The Blue Ridge Parkway is more than just a road; it is a journey in geologic time, in history, in feelings.

The geological formation of the Appalachian Mountains can be succinctly stated in two words:"creation" and "destruction." "Creation" began with uplift of rock from deep within the earth, and "destruction" continues through erosion, a slow and ongoing process. The sheer beauty of the Great Craggies lie as if a series of frozen waves with rugged eastern slopes and dramatic waterfalls while the western slopes are more gentle and host different flora and fauna. These greater elevations near the Black Mountains compose some of the tallest crests in the Blue Ridge Mountains and are fascinating, fun to clamber about, and simply breathtaking.
Photo by Frederica Georgia

Above:
Winding its way amongst the mountains, covered with colorful flowers and trees, the Blue Ridge Parkway renders finding the miraculous in something so common as a roadway an easy task. But one must consider that a work of art is not an accident; rather, it is one of inspiration, vision, and hard work. In the picture above, taken circa 1935, we have a glimpse of the road as it was before the Parkway was in place. Its planners intently fit the road to the shape of the mountains, adorned it with carefully planned stonework and landscaping, and gained hard-earned scenic easements to leave us this visual legacy, a real-life-Cinderella story.
Photo courtesy National Park Service

Below:
Children have an affinity for tunnels and these arched works of art bring out the kid in all who pass through them. There is dark mystery upon entering that soon bursts forth with brilliant light and wondrous views as "the light at the end of the tunnel." Here, a biker makes his way through one of 26 Parkway tunnels. The scalloped edges of stone, quarried nearby, form a perfect semicircular shape and are the work of stone masons from Italy and Spain. The work-intensive tunnels were modeled after the ones at the Biltmore Estate in Asheville. Local labor carried out the tedious task of drilling, blasting, removal of stone, and shoring up the sides; the process was repeated until a tunnel was formed. Tunnels, like all parts of the Parkway, were carefully planned and located to afford as little disturbance to the mountains as possible.

From the Depression
A Road to the Height of Beauty

Ralph Waldo Emerson once said, "The invariable mark of wisdom is to see the miraculous in the common." (Nature 1836) Since nature is omnipresent, sometimes it is taken for granted; however, to study nature is to be enlightened. Our environment is in perpetual motion and all one is required to do is to move with it and to feel the rhythms of the earth as old as time itself. Nothing serves up a big heaping plate of nature like the Blue Ridge Parkway, an extraordinary road that was created by visionaries during the Great Depression of the 1930s. It curves through remarkable, high mountains with vistas of wide valley expanses and hand-hewn structures built by those who passed this way years before.

The Blue Ridge Parkway is an elongated national park that was built to connect Virginia's Shenandoah and North Carolina's Great Smoky Mountains National Parks. All three parks were fully established before the end of 1935. For two years prior to the official legislation to begin the Parkway, extremely dedicated people worked to plan and begin construction as well as map the equally significant landscaping, which merged the Parkway with the environment.

Stanley W. Abbott was the resident landscape architect and first Superintendent of the Blue Ridge Parkway National Park. His son, Carlton Abbott, said of his dad, "My father and National Park Service landscape architect, Thomas Vint, were very close and they worked towards long-term preservation. Stanley Abbott would like to be remembered and appreciated for his long-term, far-reaching preservation of the Blue Ridge Parkway." Abbott, Vint, and other dedicated men sculpted this road and shaped its future, all the while believing that it could be built, even as the economy slumped and the country was steeped in one of its darkest times in history.

In a strange way, the Great Depression helped to create the Parkway because President Roosevelt and his administration were looking for worthwhile projects to provide work for the unemployed. Legend has it that while the President was touring the Civilian Conservation Corps (CCC) camps in the Shenandoah National Park on August 11, 1933, Senator Harry F. Byrd suggested a scenic drive from the Skyline Drive to the Great Smoky Mountains. The President liked the idea and, after construction commenced, he sent his White House photographer to shoot pictures so he could follow the progress.

The Blue Ridge Parkway is a road by and for humanity. It is well known for the enjoyment it offers visitors, but there have been even greater rewards from its construction. The Parkway provided work for people living in the mountains as well as for enrollees of the Civilian Conservation Corps during the Depression and later during WWII. It relieved mountain residents of their isolation due to often nonexistent or impassable roads, and it brought prosperity and hope to those thrown into the depths of the country's depressed times, allowing them access to

Craggy Gardens *(MP 363.4 to 369.6) is a mecca for visitors seeking the bountiful color in scenes prevalent in mid June. The gardens are located in the Great Craggy Mountains, one of the highest mountain ranges in the Blue Ridge. The visitor center is dedicated to nature themes, and nearby is the self-guiding trail that leads the hiker through a heady display of the alluring pinks and greens of late spring and early summer. Craggy Gardens is one of the most unique areas in the Blue Ridge Mountains in that it supports both grassy and heath balds. Scientifically, the explanation of "bald" is not clearly defined; however, these treeless areas have been categorized into two types: "grassy bald" hosting grasses, sedges, and short-growth plants; and a "heath bald" nurturing the revered rhododendron and mountain laurel.*

food and medical help. "There were people starving up here in the 1930s," mountain native and renowned Appalachian writer John Foster West stated. "For the first time, the mountain people had the hope that they could survive and no longer be so cut off from places and people that could help them with their needs."

Much of the land that now looks serene and is naturally adorned with prolific flora was originally stark, clear-cut by logging, scarred by poor farming methods, and devoid of fauna due to overhunting.

The Blue Ridge Parkway, the longest rural road in America, is the quintessential national park and a real-life Cinderella story. The National Park Service was chosen supervisor and owner of the Parkway. The Bureau of Public Roads engineered the path and worked with the Emergency Relief Administration (aka Public Works Administration) to oversee laborers who were predominantly hired locally to ease the economically depressed mountain communities. The workers helped to plant hundreds of thousands of trees and flowers, groomed the land with other landscaping, and built the amazing tunnels, overpasses, and overlooks that make a common road an object of beauty and grace.

This pleasurable drive with memorable views is portrayed in seasonal personalities including spring's verdant greens, early summer's brilliant hot pink rhododendron, blazing fall colors, and winter's bright whites embodied in crystalline sculptures of ice and snow. The Parkway beckons us to visit again and again, giving us something new and rewarding each time and another opportunity to find the miraculous in the common.

Starting at the beginning
Entering the Parkway

Entering the Parkway is akin to passing through a door where on the other side there is calm, peace, a slowed pace of living, time to walk and time to look at the beauty of landscape. Every mile says "harmony," both of the road with its surroundings and of the traveler with nature.

When the Parkway was begun in 1935, there were few deer surviving due to overhunting. Now, they are often seen at dusk grazing on grass near the road. Their gentle presence is reassuring and lends an air of wilderness.

Traveling from north to south on the following pages are a few points of interest. The visitor does not have to follow a guide to enjoy the Parkway, for there is great joy in personal discovery.

The Blue Ridge Parkway, America's favorite rural trip with its 469 curvilinear miles and 87,000 acres of pleasure driving, has become the classic example of a "parkway." Milepost 0 at **Rockfish Gap** in Virginia at the southern end of the Shenandoah National Park winds its way through undulating hills and mountains all the way to the entrance of the Great Smoky Mountains National Park at the Oconaluftee River in North Carolina. The space between is an exciting yet relaxing array of vistas with 275 overlooks, 151 bridges, 26 tunnels, and hundreds of miles of hiking trails.

This irreplaceable American treasure, the Blue Ridge Parkway, has been in the caring hands of the best engineers, landscape architects, laborers, and maintenance staff of the National Park Service since it was dedicated in 1935. Other organizations that were integral parts of the Parkway's planning include: the Bureau of Public Roads, the Forestry Service, the Cherokee Indian Agency, Veterans Administration, Civilian Conservation Corps, Public Works Administration, Civilian Public Service Administration, and the highway departments of Virginia and North Carolina.

Every intersection with public roads, concessions, and public facility has been expressly designed to give the Parkway its distinctive character. For instance, each grade was laid so that even a large motor home could manage the hills and curves with ease. Further, only one road directly intersects with the Parkway; otherwise, each junction is planned and landscaped to make as little impact possible upon the eye of the journeyman. Every interpretive sign, road sign, and milepost marker has been planned with ultimate consideration toward blending all with the environment while giving vital cultural and travel information. Access to trails and promontories are built of wood and stone. The Parkway itself is made of crushed rock that was removed to lay its path.

Humpback Rocks (MP 5-9.3) has a self-guiding trail through a collection of old Appalachian farm buildings. The rocks' humped-back appearance gives the area its name.

*As legend has it at **Yankee Horse Ridge** (MP 34.4), a hard-riding Union soldier's horse fell and had to be put down. A visitor can see the reconstructed spur of an old logging railroad by walking to Wigwam Falls.*

***James River** and the **Kanawha Canal** (MP 63.8) are built with a footbridge across the river to the restored canal locks. A self-guiding trail follows the river bluff and offers an explanation of the lock system (right).*

The lowest point on the Parkway
Crossing the James River

A visitor center greets Parkway travelers at the James River at 649 feet above sea level, the lowest point along this scenic drive. Interpretive exhibits tell of early transportation and the importance of the James River and its system of locks for moving goods from plantations and Richmond to the Blue Ridge area and westward. On the south side of the bridge are restored portions of the locks.

The power of water is evident here as millions of years of erosion have formed the beautiful river and boundaries of the **James River Water Gap**. A hiking trail threads through identified trees including giant white oaks, red oaks with multi-fingered leaves, pawpaws, hackberries, and oak chestnuts that thrive on the edge of a flood plain. Roots of some trees grow literally out of rock, exhibiting one way that new soil is formed to give footing for other plants.

The **James River Bridge** (MP 63.6) witnesses the prescience of Parkway planners: the road above is a path for vehicles and bicycles, while the footbridge below spans the river for the pedestrian looking for a more personal experience.

A resort area since the days of Thomas Jefferson
Peaks of Otter

This idyllic scene along the Parkway in Virginia takes the traveler to the Peaks of Otter. The reasons are obvious as to why travelers, as early as the nineteenth century, have journeyed great distances to reach the mountains, a well of serenity.

*An ancient apple tree, silhouetted in the setting sun, is located by **Abbott Lake** in back of the **Peaks of Otter Lodge** (below). Since the days of Thomas Jefferson, travelers seeking the solace of a mountain setting have been vacationing in this area. The lake is named for Stanley W. Abbott, revered National Park Service resident landscape architect and its first superintendent during construction in the 1930s. The lodge is the only year-round concessioner on the Parkway.*

*A National Park Service summer interpreter is dressed in period clothing to greet visitors and relate family life on the **Johnson farm**. The farm is across the Parkway from the Peaks of Otter.*

A fence museum
Groundhog Mountain

Pioneer building was often rustic and accomplished with few tools and materials that were readily available. Trees were felled, stripped of bark, then hand-hewn into practical planking. Cabins were often small with perhaps four rooms. Fences were of the same type of construction with different types reflecting the needs of the individual. On **Groundhog Mountain** (MP 188.8), there is a display of four types of fencing used by pioneers to border property, corral stock animals, or surround the yard to keep other animals out. Now, residents along the Parkway are encouraged to fence their property for both esthetic and useful reasons. The fencing along the scenic drive is picturesque with its origins from the first days of mountaineers' presence in the Blue Ridge Mountains.

Groundhog Mountain offers a close-up look at fencing used in the mountains. Most fences seen on the Parkway were built of chestnut. This area is a lovely place to stroll around the meadow, picnic, and to climb the observation tower and contemplate the charming hillside and small graveyard nearby.

Four prevalent **types of fencing** *were used in the Blue Ridge Mountains. Above top, right of page is the "buck" fence. The angles of the boards held each to the other; above is the "post and rail" fence; lower, far right is the "picket" or "paling" fence style, and finally, at right the "snake" fence.*

Fields of cabbage, a classic Irish staple, adorn the Parkway in fields of cool green. This cold-weather-loving vegetable remains a dependable cash crop and favorite dish.
Photo by Frederica Georgia

Time moves slowly up here
A Land of Small Mountain Farms

By the 1930s, when the timbering business had invaded the mountains, railroads had tracked their way through many areas, and the Blue Ridge Parkway construction had begun, life for mountaineers had changed forever. No longer was the isolated mountain resident the stereotype, for farming, as a way to self-sufficiency, had become mixed with public jobs and tourism as a means of support for many mountain families.

Today, thanks to scenic easements that allow the National Park Service to restrict the use of land along the Parkway, a visitor can still see how mountain residents lived. The quaint, small farms were means of survival where vegetables were raised, animals kept for produce, and special crops, including burley tobacco and cabbage, were cultivated for cash. As a means of subsistence, communities formed and various families offered special services such as establishing a mill to grind corn into flour and grits. Alone, a family might perish should a growing season be unkind, but, as a community, families worked together to progressively lessen the amount of work each one had to do and, at the same time, took advantage of advancing technology.

Pioneers introduced apples, peaches, and pears to the Blue Ridge Mountains. In a scene much unchanged over the years, this old apple tree hangs over a wooden fence at a small mountain farm. The apple was a diverse fruit that could be used to bake pies or make apple butter, a traditional recipe brought to the area by German settlers.

A Blue Ridge Parkway visitor was overhead to say, "I like the Mabry Mill Trail the best because there is so much to do there." With a restaurant and book/gift shop, it is a popular stop for casual travelers as well as those seeking a day of activities. Photographic opportunities abound with rustic settings scattered throughout the site.

An artist's dream
Mabry Mill

Mabry Mill (MP 176) is one of the most photographed sites along the Blue Ridge Parkway. Ed and Lizzie Mabry, original owners of the much-loved mill, likely never anticipated that their hard work would become considered a work of art and a lasting example of the mountain resident's self-sufficiency. The mill's design also earns the well-deserved admiration of engineers with its flutes that funnel the water from several sources directly to the waterwheel. Seasoned by the rigors of West Virginia coal mining, Ed Mabry came to the Blue Ridge Mountains with the jack-of-all-trade skills needed to survive in a world where nature challenged every man's ingenuity.

Around 1910, Ed built a gristmill, sawmill, and wheelwright shop to serve the community of Meadows of Dan. Like all grist mills, it was a place families gathered and children played games while waiting for their grain to be milled. Nearby was their two-story wooden frame house, typical architecture of around 1900. The original house was later moved and replaced by a log cabin in the 1950s when the National Park Service was attempting to represent the log cabin era of mountain living.

Ed worked the mill for over two dozen years until his health began to fail. Upon his death in 1936, the mill fell into disrepair. Despite its rough appearance, however, National Park Service landscape architects recognized its beauty when

Mabry Mill is one of the most picturesque scenes in America. The old wooden mill, set by water in fall color, is an artist's dream. When building the Parkway, National Park Service resident landscape architect, Stanley W. Abbott, recognized the historic significance of saving the mill. Today during summers, wood smoke rises from a woodshed where the chinking sound of an anvil on iron is heard as a blacksmith demonstrates his skill just as Ed Mabry would have done while fashioning a wagon wheel for a neighbor.

building the Parkway and secured the property for future restoration and preservation.

Today, with a restaurant and gift shop, it is one of the busiest sites along the Blue Ridge Parkway. Mabry Mill is a living historic district hosting scheduled demonstrations of blacksmithing and molasses and apple butter making during summer and fall. In less than a one-half mile leisurely walk, the Mountain Industry Trail fills the senses with a variety of experiences. Along this brief hike, there are restored buildings, typical farm implements, an old field wagon, and other displays which the National Park Service has preserved with the intent to portray rural life in the Blue Ridge Mountains.

Photo Pinpoints & Popular Places Along the Blue Ridge Parkway

MP 451.2 **Waterrock Knob Overlook** with its paved parking area and a small visitor center just off the Parkway provides panoramic views. Sunrise and sunset can be spectacular.

MP 339.5 **Crabtree Meadows and Falls** has a campground, restaurant, gift shop, and self-guiding trails to the waterfalls, a photographer's dream.

MP 316.3 **Linville Falls** takes a spectacular plunge here. From the visitor center, self-guiding trails offer the best views of one of the most famous waterfalls in the Blue Ridge Mountains.

MP 295.1 - 298 **Julian Price Memorial Park** is comprised of a beautiful lake and a number of hiking trails.

MP 241.1 **Doughton Park Campground** and area includes the lodge, restaurant, gas station, nearby are the Brinegar and Caudill Cabins and trails. Enjoy a night at a cozy lodge with an outd

MP 411-416 near **Wagon Road Gap**. Nearby overlooks are where Monarch butterflies can be seen crossing the Parkway in September.

MP 363.4 - 369.6 **Craggy Gardens** is an unforgettable experience with a visitor center, gift shop, and hiking trails. During mid-June, the catawba rhododendron cover the mountainside with blooms.

MP 305.1 **Grandfather Mountain** is privately owned and reached by a private road to the top. Exit the Parkway onto US 221. There is an entrance fee to reach the year-round wildlife preserve, museum, and famous swinging bridge at the top of the mountain.

MP 258.6 **Northwest Trading Post** is sponsored by the Northwest Development Association to keep alive the old crafts of the Blue Ridge Mountains. There are home-baked goodies, crafts, old-time toys and quilts. The adjacent Eastern National store has books, videos, and restrooms.

MP 272 **E.B. Jeffress Park** offers a self-guiding trail to cascades, and another to an old cabin and church.

MP 431.4 **Richland Balsam Overlook** boasts the highest point on the Parkway with elevation at 6,047 feet.

MP 408.6 **Mount Pisgah** is a famous mountain retreat that has an inn, restaurant, campground and camp store, gas station, and gift shop. Once a part of the Biltmore Estate, the rooms have balconies with memorable views; phone (828) 235-8228.

MP 382 **The Folk Art Center** is a cooperative venture between the National Park Service and the Southern Highland Handicraft Guild. A great selection of crafts and books along with interpretive programs and exhibits are available. There is also a visitor center.

MP 458.2 **Heintooga Ridge** has a spur road that leads to a mile-high overlook, just 1.3 miles from the Parkway.

MP 418.8 **Graveyard Fields Overlook** offers self-guiding trails to several beautiful waterfalls.

MP 469 **The Great Smoky Mountain National Park** is the southern bookend for the Blue Ridge Parkway, just north of Cherokee.

MP 355.4 **Mt. Mitchell State Park** is home to the highest mountain east of the Mississippi and has a state park, lookout tower, and restaurant at the top.

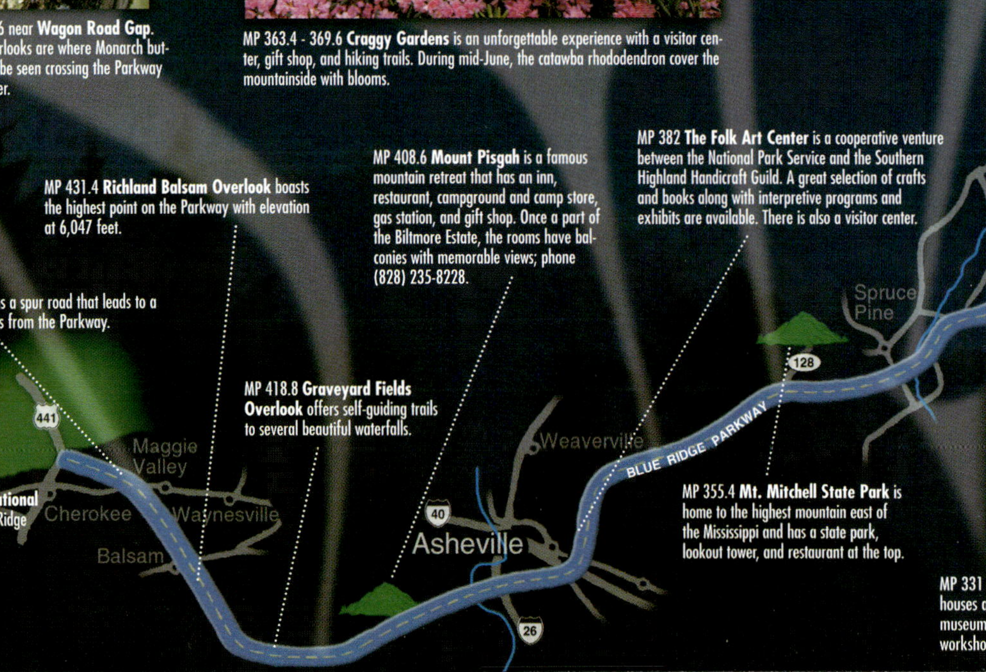

MP 331 **Museum of North Carolina Minerals** and visitor center houses an amazing variety of minerals and gemstones displayed in a museum that has been expanded. Nearby are area rock shops and workshops kept by craftsmen and well-known artisans.

 Skyline Drive Charlottesville

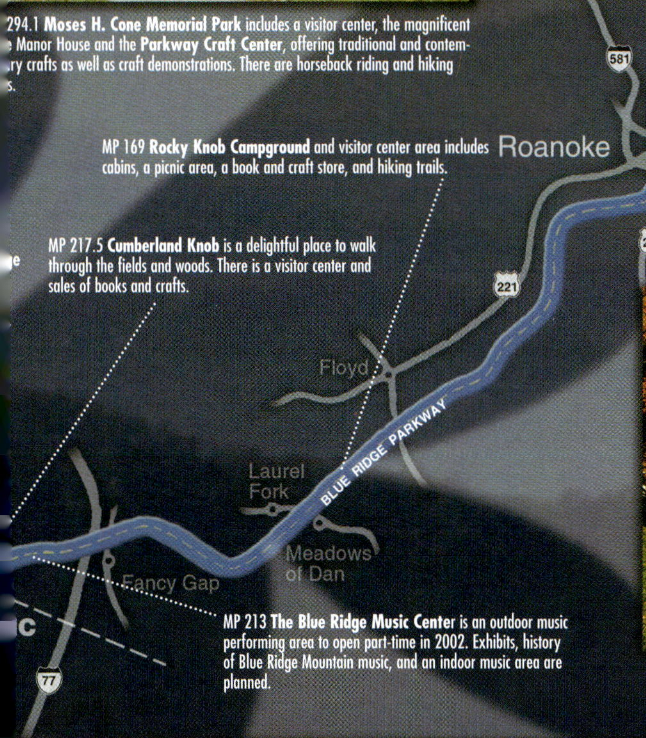

MP 34.4 **Yankee Horse Ridge** is the place where legend says, a hard riding Union soldier's horse fell. There also is an old logging railroad reconstruction.

MP 0 **Rockfish Gap** is the northern bookend of the Blue Ridge Parkway where it meets Skyline Drive, the boundary of the Shenandoah National Park and intersects with I-64.

294.1 **Moses H. Cone Memorial Park** includes a visitor center, the magnificent Manor House and the **Parkway Craft Center**, offering traditional and contemporary crafts as well as craft demonstrations. There are horseback riding and hiking...

MP 6.1 **Humpback Rocks** has old and quaint Appalachian farm buildings, a short hiking trail, and visitor center.

MP 169 **Rocky Knob Campground** and visitor center area includes cabins, a picnic area, a book and craft store, and hiking trails.

MP 115 **Virginia's Explore Park** and historic **Brugh Tavern** offer meals in a historic setting. There is a welcome center/museum amidst an 1100-acre-outdoor-living-history area with costumed interpretation.

MP 60.9 - 63.8 **Otter Creek Campground** is a good stop with a restaurant, visitor center, and an interesting gift shop. From here, the 3.5 mile Otter Creek Trail winds down to the **James River Visitor Center** and the **Kanawha Canal Lock** with a walkway bridge over the river and under the Parkway.

MP 217.5 **Cumberland Knob** is a delightful place to walk through the fields and woods. There is a visitor center and sales of books and crafts.

MP 213 **The Blue Ridge Music Center** is an outdoor music performing area to open part-time in 2002. Exhibits, history of Blue Ridge Mountain music, and an indoor music area are planned.

MP 176.1 **Mabry Mill** is famous for its gristmill. It is likely the most photographed scene along the Parkway with its sawmill, blacksmith shop, restaurant, and book and crafts shop.

MP 84 - 87 **Peaks of Otter** Lodge and restaurant overlook Abbott Lake (phone [540] 586-1081 for reservations- highly suggested). Nearby are the **Johnson Farm**, and the historic **Polly Woods Ordinary**. Along with a visitor center, gas station, hiking trails, campground and store, and RV/trailer sites, this is one of the most interesting stops on the Parkway.

MP 188.8 **Groundhog Mountain** and recreation area demonstrates the types of fences found along the Blue Ridge Parkway. There is an observation tower, picnic area, and restrooms.

Notes: All visitor centers have restroom facilities. For general information including Parkway road conditions, call (828) 298-0398 or visit the Blue Ridge Parkway on the web at www.blueridgeparkway.org.

The Parkway is marked every mile by concrete mileposts beginning at MP 0 in Virginia and ending at MP 469 at the Great Smoky Mountain National Park.

Other recommended overlooks:
MP 10.7 Raven's Roost
MP 38.8 Boston Knob
MP 95.3 Harvey's Knob
MP 168 The Saddle
MP 266.9 Mount Jefferson Overlook
MP 310 Lost Cove Cliffs
MP 415.7 Cherry Cove
MP 422.4 Devil's Courthouse

A toe-tappin' event
Mountain Music and Dance

One of the most delightful experiences along the Parkway can be enjoyed on Sundays in summer and fall at **Mabry Mill** when the park sponsors a mountain music session in its quest to preserve local culture. Musicians gather to play traditional mountain music for all to hear. It is refreshing and exhilarating to watch and hear the musicians jam on hammered and lap dulcimer, fiddle, banjo, guitar, mandolin, autoharp, and bass. Recalling traditions from their colonial ancestry, local residents join in with time-honored music and dance as depicted in the photographs above, taken at Mabry Mill in fall 2001.

The old and the young dance alone or together while visiting grandchildren are eventually lured to the dance platform to do some toe tappin' and clogging. Appalachian clogging is a blend of dances: jigs brought by early Irish and Scottish settlers, clogging from the British, a high-kicking buck dance from African Americans, and the stomp that may have come from American Indian influence. Though the mountain dancing has been called "flatfooting," "step dancing," "hoe-downing," or "back stepping," the old mountaineers just call it "dancing."

Mountain music reflects the homeland traditions of early settlers in the region. Immigrants to the Appalachians with European roots, mostly Scotch-Irish, English, and German, brought with them their ballads and tunes along with the fiddle (violin). The banjo was introduced by West Africans and was soon adopted in the stringband ensemble as accompaniment to songs and ballads. It was commonplace in the Blue Ridge by the nineteenth century though few African Americans lived in the region at that time.

Because early travel was often limited to familiar territory, each community had its own style, distinctions that continue to be heard today. It was only when travelers and settlers ventured to the "wilderness," as the mountains were known during the eighteenth and nineteenth centuries, that young musicians learned from other masters, exchanging and blending repertoires and playing styles.

Whatever the style and origins, music was and still is an integral part of the lives of those who have settled in the Blue Ridge Mountains. As Marshall Wyatt observes in his notes to the recording *Music from the Lost Provinces*, "It was a social music that celebrated local events and provided diversion from hard work, a music that created bonds between neighbors and served as a link from one generation to the next."

On summer and fall Sundays, the tradition continues. A clapping, smiling audience joins the fun as they marvel at the sheer talent of these resourceful folks. Neighbors greet neighbors while lucky visitors rub shoulders with descendants of resilient mountain pioneers.

The young dancer, with a Mona Lisa smile in the picture above, holds the secrets of traditional mountain music and dance shared with her by generations of Blue Ridge Mountain families.

The National Park Service in cooperation with the National Council for the Traditional Arts has designed The Blue Ridge Music Center on the Parkway near Galax, Virginia, to pay tribute to the rich musical heritage of the Blue Ridge.

An original loom demonstration
Brinegar Cabin

Upon visiting the **Brinegar Cabin** (MP 238.5), one can still feel the lingering spirits of Caroline and Martin Brinegar who lived here beginning in the late 1800s until Caroline, widowed in 1925, moved due to Parkway construction in 1935. Legend has it that she wove linen and wool cloth on a loom similar to the one on display within the cabin. The Brinegars were typical examples of the self-supporting mountain family who built their own log cabin from hand-hewn timber, a barn in which to house the large family of animals including cows and chickens, and planted various crops for their own use such as corn, vegetables, and flax.

Brinegar descendants gather at the cabin each year, continuing the ever-present spirit of this enduring mountain family. There are walking trails and an exhibit with examples of the crops that Caroline and Martin cultivated. The preserved cabin, set amidst gardens and forest, represents the sturdy character of mountain residents.

The **Julian Price Memorial Park** (MP 296.7), a leviathan 3,900-acre area, was donated to the National Park Service in 1949 by Price's children, Ralph Clay and Kathleen. Price had been founder, president and chairman of the board of two insurance companies in Greensboro that became the merged Jefferson-Pilot Insurance Company.

Price's children asked that a dam be erected on the estate to establish a lake, their father's dream, in exchange for the donation of the land to the park. The result is Price Lake, a beautiful manmade reservoir, completed for the public's pleasure. The Price family's philanthropy lives on in the park's beauty where visitors can enjoy hiking, canoeing, fishing, picnicking, and camping.

A place for fishing
Price Lake

Price Lake (above) is blanketed in the morning mist. Fishermen enjoy the 47-acre lake, thanks to the Julian Price family who gave the estate to the National Park Service in 1949. It is just one of many niches along the Parkway that helps us return to nature and enjoy quietude.
Photo by Frederica Georgia

Brinegar's Cabin (left) is an enduring example of one type of mountain architecture. Frame houses had largely replaced log cabins by 1900. Inside is a loom, said to have been used by Caroline Brinegar to weave wool and linen. It is easy to imagine her and husband Martin's presence as there are exhibits explaining how this self-sufficient family survived.

A mansion and craft center, horseback riding, and hiking trails
Moses H. Cone Memorial Park

Moses H. Cone was the eldest of thirteen children, all of rugged German descent. A young entrepreneur, he and brother Caesar established the hugely-successful Cone Mills that began in Greensboro. Fascinated with the Appalachian Mountains as a place he could improve his often-poor health, he and wife Bertha built the twenty-room **Flat Top Manor** (MP 294), the finest example of Neo-Colonial architecture in North Carolina. A visitor may think that Cone led a retired life, but nothing could be further from the truth. Cone created many industrious and ecologically-minded projects such as establishing 25 miles of horse carriage trails, cultivating a one-of-a-kind 10,000 apple tree orchard, building two lakes and stocking them with native bass and trout, and, with his wife, beautifying the environment all around Flat Top Manor, even importing deer to refresh the dwindling numbers.

After Bertha Cone's death, the 3,517-acre estate went to the Moses H. Cone Hospital in Greensboro and subsequently was bequeathed to the Blue Ridge Parkway in 1949. Flat Top Manor, a "mansion in the sky" is part of the Moses H. Cone Memorial Park and offers a variety of exhibits and recreation. Today, there are hiking trails, horseback riding, scheduled arts and crafts demonstrations, and the Parkway Craft Center, operated by the Southern Highland Craft Guild, an association that preserves traditional mountain crafts as well as contemporary creations.

The donation of the Cone and Price estates added a tremendous boost to the preservation of the Blue Ridge environment and represents the great talent, arduous efforts, and good will that came together at the right time to create this magnificent national park.

*Around 1900, Moses Cone sought a restful place where he could improve his health and serve as a summer mansion. He and wife Bertha bought land in the Boone and Blowing Rock areas including Flat Top and Rich Mountains and soon began building their estate. **Flat Top Manor** became a cultivation center for Cone's industrious ideas like his beloved apple trees and orchids. Today, it continues as a haven for the naturalist, historian, and outdoorsman. Within the beautiful home is the friendly and warm Parkway Craft Center, operated by the Southern Highland Craft Guild, and a National Park Service visitor center.*

There are 25 miles of horse trails in the Moses H. Cone Memorial Park, originally built as carriage trails for access to the apple orchards and outbuildings on the estate. One trail leads from the privately owned stables past the 20-room Flat Top Manor and down past the carriage house. The thrill of a high altitude ride, sauntering past remnants of Cone's gardens and apple trees, is a memorable trek. The fresh mountain air, the sun's warmth, and a horse easing down a lane are relaxing, renewing experiences.

*In the **Museum of North Carolina Minerals**, samples such as blue aquamarine, a variety of "beryl," can be seen (picture at right). The surrounding area includes Spruce Pine and Little Switzerland, famous for mica as well as emeralds and other minerals and gemstones.*

A Parkway museum for viewing geology
Rocks and Minerals

The **Museum of North Carolina Minerals** (MP 331) offers an impressive display of rocks and minerals, which includes amphibolite, quartz, biotite mica, and garnet. National Park Service rangers who are versed in mountain geology answer questions and offer up tidbits of interest like the fact that garnet was crushed and used to pave the Parkway. Nearby is Spruce Pine, famous for feldspar, mica, and other minerals. Emeralds are also found nearby. Another place to see impressive rocks and minerals such as amethyst, smoky quartz, and other gemstones is in the museum aloft at Grandfather Mountain.

North Carolina was once the site of a gold rush and in the western mountains, rubies and emeralds have been mined. This is the result of millions of years of upheaval of newer material deep within the earth's furnace, metamorphosing existing rock into gemstones, making many areas of the mountains a rockhound's haven.

The area from Little Switzerland to Spruce Pine has many rock shops and crafts by local artisans along the local roads. The Mitchell County Chamber of Commerce has an office within the Museum of North Carolina Minerals and can suggest where to stay and what to see. It is a memorable experience to see the wealth of gemstones at this center and touch time locked within the crystals on display.

Saving the View for the Future
By Hugh Morton, Owner Grandfather Mountain

North Carolina recognizes that the Blue Ridge Parkway is one of its great assets, and two organizations to which I belonged had leadership roles in rallying protection for the Parkway. Western North Carolina Tomorrow, a regional leadership group sponsored by Western Carolina University, led the way for passage in the General Assembly of the Ridge Law, which limits the height of buildings that can be constructed on ridges 3000 feet or more in elevation. The same WNC Tomorrow group has been in the forefront to combat air pollution, the Number One threat to the Mountains.

The Governor of North Carolina in 1995 appointed the Year of the Mountains commission to give additional thrust to several projects advanced by WNC Tomorrow. Among the most important was consolidation of support for additional right of way for the Blue Ridge Parkway where existing right of way was insufficient. A great many individuals, government agencies, and organizations became a part of the effort generated by the Year of the Mountains, and by the year 2002 the campaign had added more than 26,000 acres of protection for the Parkway via purchase, donation, and conservation easement. This program continues, conducted by the Conservation Trust for North Carolina whose office is in Raleigh.

One of the most famous pictures taken along the Parkway is this fawn in the forest on Grandfather Mountain. The little-known story behind this image follows. The mother doe, which could only take care of one of her twins, had abandoned the fawn. Subsequently, the twin died, and after raising the fawn on a bottle, Hugh Morton successfully returned this little one to its mother.
Photo by Hugh Morton

Driving the Blue Ridge Parkway is like hearing the refrain of an old, favorite tune. The scenic road perpetually plays Nature's song, written in rhythms and soothing notes that touch the soul.

The Linn Cove Viaduct- an engineering marvel
The Parkway Completed

With the same flair and flourish with which it was begun in 1935, the Blue Ridge Parkway was finally completed in 1987. The National Park Service had to wait twenty years to plan and build the final bridge, the **Linn Cove Viaduct** (MP 304.4), to complete the seamless Parkway linking the Shenandoah and Great Smoky Mountain National Parks. Construction had halted in 1967 until the last 7.5 miles could be completed, which included a bridge around a fragile part of Grandfather Mountain. The geological significance of this particular area called for an all-new bridge design to skirt the rocky perimeter of Grandfather Mountain. Once again, the park and its engineers not only accomplished the feat but also did it in keeping with the esthetic philosophy with which the Parkway had been created half a century earlier.

After many debates, a path for the viaduct was decided upon. Next, engineers were hired to develop a design/build method for the 1,243-foot-long, pre-cast concrete bridge. With a dramatic building technique, the 153 segments, weighing 50 tons each, were connected by a stiff-leg crane and secured to the next section with epoxy. Steel cables within each section conjoined one with the next rendering the S-curved bridge as if one entity. The first section that was put in place served as the only construction platform, eliminating a construction access road and other infringements upon nature. Only the pier foundations touched the mountain and landscaping repaired any scars left by the support placement. Minimizing the degree of visual impact of manmade structures upon the environment has always been a significant theme to Parkway designers; therefore, the bridge's concrete was tinted with iron oxide.

This last part of the Parkway, completed between 1968-1987, was one of the most challenging as it included 12 bridges, 12 overlooks, and the Tanawha Trail that connects Beacon Heights to the Julian Price Memorial Park. What a grand conclusion this was for the Parkway, offering striking vistas at numerous turns.

Completing the Blue Ridge Parkway is tantamount to offering the ultimate gift of nature to visitors, for Nature is enlightenment. It is in perpetual motion and all one must do is stand for a moment and feel the rhythms of the earth as old as time itself. The Parkway is a sanctuary for animals and trees, a place for peace, grand vistas, and hikes that are leisurely or challenging. Sprinkled throughout the road's course, on and off the Parkway, are a variety of shops and small communities with their own flavor.

Completed in 1987, the Blue Ridge Parkway became a seamless 469-mile scenic drive from the Shenandoah National Park in Virginia to the magnificent Great Smoky Mountains National Park in the western mountains of North Carolina. The S-curve of the Linn Cove Viaduct slips around one edge of Grandfather Mountain as smoothly as the sweep of the second hand on the face of a clock.
Photos by Hugh Morton

*A uniquely designed concrete bridge, the **Linn Cove Viaduct** is an engineering triumph. Only its foundation piers touch **Grandfather Mountain** and the construction technique that was used allowed it to be built from the top down, thus minimizing impact on the 800-million-years-old mountain, one of the oldest mountains in the world. To reach Grandfather Mountain, exit off the Parkway onto US 221 to the private toll road to the top where there are exhibits and the famous mile-high swinging bridge. It is considered the most biologically diverse mountain in eastern North America. The area is full of amazing vistas where the only thing to stop the traveler is the horizon*
Photo by Hugh Morton

Crabtree Falls, part of *Crabtree Meadows*, is one of the most famous waterfalls on the Blue Ridge Parkway and certainly is one of the most photographed. It is a short walk from the Crabtree Meadows parking lot and campground. The falling water cascades off dozens of rocks on the way down, offering a spectacular photo opportunity. Also, several streams splash right beside the Parkway, creating a refreshing, soothing encounter for visitors. Even the hardiest hiker can appreciate the loop trail, appointed with spring wildflowers and early summer rhododendron that add to the magnificent visual experience.

The most popular Parkway Waterfalls

Two of the most spectacular waterfalls along the Blue Ridge Parkway in North Carolina are **Linville Falls** (MP 316.4) and **Crabtree Falls** (MP 339.5). Also, one of the most visited is at **Graveyard Fields** (MP 418.8). The following information will give the traveler an idea of where some of the most popular Parkway waterfalls can be located.

Linville Falls, near Grandfather Mountain and perhaps the best known waterfall on the Parkway, offers two areas of interest in its upper and lower falls. Two main hiking trails lead from the visitor center to the falls while meandering through remnants of a hemlock forest. From the time one steps onto the shaded path, nerves begin to calm and the mind to relax. Then there is the sound of the water approaching closer and closer; the cool, tumbling water is like balm for the soul. The Erwins View Trail, a moderate hike of 1.6-mile roundtrip, affords four different views of both the upper and lower falls. This well-loved area is made to walk awhile and stop awhile. It's guaranteed to leave the hiker feeling refreshed and renewed.

A second trail leaves the visitor center and heads toward **Linville Gorge** and **Plunge Basin Overlook**. This trail is more strenuous, stretching 1.4 miles, and has a branch off the trail dropping down the steep side of the wall surrounding the falls. Though demanding, the trail affords an exhilarating experience with the plunging, rushing waters from Linville Falls.

At **Crabtree Falls**, near Little Switzerland, where the trail leads to the base of the falls, a hiker should allow about two hours to cover the 2.6-mile-loop trail from the parking lot to the waterfall. Photographers particularly like these falls because the water dramatically splashes off the rocks as it hits below and provides excellent photo opportunities.

Looking Glass Falls is located only a few miles off the Parkway at the intersection with US Highway 276 near Brevard, North Carolina, at Wagongap Road (MP 411.8) within Pisgah National Forest. The falls are visible from the highway and the base of the falls can be reached by a path just a few hundred feet long. This classic waterfall has appeared in many travel and vacation publications. On the other side of the highway in this same area is **Sliding Rock**. Within the Pisgah National Forest, visitors are allowed to enjoy the natural rockslide. Long before man-made waterslides were built, kids of early settlers were using this natural waterslide tucked within the cool shade of the Blue Ridge Mountain.

In Virginia, the most noteworthy waterfall is **Fallingwater Cascades** (MP 83.4). It can be seen along a 1.6-mile-loop trail. Stone steps descend to Fallingwater Creek while a footbridge at the beginning of the 200-foot cascades affords the hiker a look at this unique spot.

*There are three waterfalls in **Graveyard Fields** (MP 418.8): Upper, Second, and Yellowstone Falls. From the large parking area, different paths lead to different waterfalls; the easiest walk is to Second Falls. "Graveyard Fields" received its name in 1925 when a devastating fire burned the magnificent, green forest and left tree stumps looking like gravestones. In more than three-quarters of a century since the fire, nature has healed much of the damage. The trail to Upper Falls is flat and pleasurable for the most part, but the last stretch is quite a climb. All three trails are fascinating, each one beginning in a dense growth of rhododendron and then changing as the terrain changes. Exploring the falls of Graveyard Fields is exemplary of the rich and diverse experience on the Blue Ridge Parkway because even within the same day of the same season, terrain and flora change right before the traveler's eyes. This is certainly one reason this area of the Parkway remains very popular.*
Photo by Frederica Georgia

***Linville Falls**, one of the most famous waterfalls in Western North Carolina, continues to captivate hundreds of thousands of visitors each year. Pictured at right is the plunging lower falls and, at a greater elevation (barely discernible), the dramatic upper falls. During the flood of 1916, when nearly two feet of rain fell over 24 consecutive hours, the configuration of the upper falls was dramatically and forever changed, taking nearly one-half of the fall's height by carrying away the rocky shelf over which the Linville River flowed. Known as the "Great Flood of 1916," the deluge of rain inundated mountain residents and presented them with a great challenge to survive. Today, Linville Falls is known for its solace, created by a tidal wash of water over these ancient rocks.*

Traditional toys and crafts
Simple Joys and Toys of the Blue Ridge

In the years before the Blue Ridge Parkway opened the area to visitors, toys, musical instruments, thrown pottery, and indeed all devices needed to survive, were handmade of natural materials available nearby. Each mountain resident brought to the Blue Ridge Mountains crafts from European ancestry. With the skill of fine craftsmanship, hammered and lap dulcimers (pictured below) were made of maple and cherry and were played with a hickory pick. Dolls were made of corn shucks and toys like "whirrlygigs" and the "ball and cup" were made of wood and sticks.

Wooden toys that had simple moving parts often imitated life such as chickens pecking corn and the dancing man. Other toys like stilts made from tree limbs, wooden wagons, and hand-whittled whistles were uncomplicated but provided great entertainment.

Some of these long-established toys and mountain crafts, which continue to fascinate kids of all ages, are still sold at the Northwest Trading Post, the craft centers, and other locations along the Parkway. Each traditional toy, music instrument, and craft celebrates the rich cultural heritage of mountain pioneers.

During any season, a visitor can find special places to stop. For example, farms situated near the Parkway often sell pumpkins in the fall. This young lady has found just the right one to take home.

Ed Presnell made this dulcimer in the 1960s. He lived on a mountain near Banner Elk, where this picture was taken, and became legendary for the quality of his instruments.

Mountain crafts, steeped in tradition, were designed for practicality as well as entertainment. Quilting provided warmth, decoration, and socialization. A quilt's patchwork of symbols spoke of people, of family and home, of community and friendship. Pioneer women often traded scraps of cloth and patterns; they met to help one another and shared family news, parenting tips, and home remedies. A quilt literally had all the elements of culture stitched into its beautiful design that often carried even deeper meaning in popular patterns including the "Double Wedding Ring, or "Jacob's Ladder." The quilts pictured above were made by Daisy Ward of Bakersville, NC. The first one from left is "Skip Around the Mountain." The second and third quilts from left are variations of "Bear's Paw," and the second one from right is "Black Diamond." Quilt patterns were handed down as a tradition; however, quilters took pride in personalized designs that harbored the artist's secrets in its tessellations.

Mountain girls preferred corn-shuck dolls (right) while the boys spent hours trying to get the ball in the cup (above) - not as easy as it appears!

A true winter wonderland and spring returns
The Parkway in Winter

Snow and ice turn the Parkway into a winter wonderland near Asheville. Sections of the Blue Ridge Parkway close during the winter due to snow or storm damage. However, these sections may be open to hikers, sledders, and cross country skiers, giving them the opportunity to explore stunning winter scenes. For more information on road conditions, call (828) 298-0398.

Three ranges, the Pisgah Ledge, the Great Balsams, and the Plott Balsams lead into the Great Smokies. Winter reaches intense levels and often closes the portions of the Parkway above 5,000 feet; however, foggy sunrises and blankets of clouds in the valleys make for some of the grandest panoramas available in the East.

One of the beauties of the Parkway is that the traveler can watch the seasons move up and down the mountains. Spring begins at the lower elevations and moves upward. Fall is just the opposite, peaking first at higher elevations and lingering at the lower elevations and in protected coves. The frigid season can encroach quickly, though, since higher elevations yield cooler temperatures, persistent winds, and changeable weather. Winter seems to bring everything to a standstill on the Parkway; however, growth continues in the earth's fine crust. Spotting a trillium in spring, awakened from the depths of cold, is memorable as time completes one cycle and begins another.